CU00497242

COSMIC CUISINE: THE SCIENCE BEHIND ASTRONAUT FOOD AND SPACE AGRICULTURE

A Journey through the Evolution, Challenges, and Future of Dining in the Cosmos

D.R. T STEPHENS

S.D.N Publishing

CONTENTS

GENERAL DISCLAIMER

This book is intended to provide informative and educational material on the subject matter covered. The author(s), publisher, and any affiliated parties make no representations or warranties with respect to the accuracy, applicability, completeness, or suitability of the contents herein and specifically disclaim any implied warranties of merchantability or fitness for a particular purpose.

The information contained in this book is for general information purposes only and is not intended to serve as legal, medical, financial, or any other form of professional advice. Readers should consult with appropriate professionals before making any decisions based on the information provided. Neither the author(s) nor the publisher shall be held responsible or liable for any loss, damage, injury, claim, or otherwise, whether direct or indirect, consequential, or incidental, that may occur as a result of applying or misinterpreting the information in this book.

This book may contain references to third-party websites, products, or services. Such references do not constitute an endorsement or recommendation, and the author(s) and publisher are not responsible for any outcomes related to these third-party references.

In no event shall the author(s), publisher, or any affiliated parties be liable for any direct, indirect, punitive, special, incidental, or other consequential damages arising directly or indirectly from any use of this material, which is provided "as is," and without warranties of any kind, express or implied.

By reading this book, you acknowledge and agree that you assume all risks and responsibilities concerning the applicability and consequences of the information provided. You also agree to indemnify, defend, and hold harmless the author(s), publisher, and any affiliated parties from any and all liabilities, claims, demands, actions, and causes of action whatsoever, whether or not foreseeable, that may arise from using or misusing the information contained in this book.

Although every effort has been made to ensure the accuracy of the information in this book as of the date of publication, the landscape of the subject matter covered is continuously evolving. Therefore, the author(s) and publisher expressly disclaim responsibility for any errors or omissions and reserve the right to update, alter, or revise the content without prior notice.

By continuing to read this book, you agree to be bound by the terms and conditions stated in this disclaimer. If you do not agree with these terms, it is your responsibility to discontinue use of this book immediately.

CHAPTER 1: AN APPETITE FOR THE INFINITE: INTRODUCTION TO SPACE NUTRITION

As we cast our eyes upwards and reach outwards into the vast expanse of the cosmos, one of the most fundamental human needs remains - nourishment. No matter how far we venture into the unknown, our biological requirement for nutrients will always follow. This is the intriguing premise of space nutrition, an evolving discipline born from the marriage of human curiosity and the inescapable biology of our species.

The nature of space - with its microgravity, radiation, and other environmental challenges - presents unique problems for human nutrition. A simple act of eating a meal becomes a ballet of floating food particles and escaping liquids while our bodies respond in unexpected ways to this otherworldly setting. Food, therefore, isn't just sustenance in space; it's a science, a comfort, a challenge, and a field of study that yields vital insights into human health and well-being.

Understanding space nutrition begins by recognizing the key role of nutrients - proteins, carbohydrates, fats, vitamins, and minerals - in human health. Nutrients fuel our bodies, repair damaged cells, and support the growth of new ones. On Earth, these processes take place under the relentless pull of gravity, a force that subtly but profoundly influences how our bodies function.

However, in space, gravity is practically absent. This microgravity environment alters how our bodies process nutrients. Bone density changes, muscle mass decreases, and fluid distribution shifts - all are influenced by the gravity, or lack thereof, in our environment. Space nutrition must account for these alterations and adjust diets accordingly to ensure astronauts' health and well-being.

Moreover, space nutrition isn't just about the individual nutrients and their absorption in the human body. It encompasses the entire process from meal selection and packaging on Earth to storage and preparation in space to consumption and disposal of waste. Every step in this chain is uniquely complicated by the space environment and requires creative and often surprising solutions.

As we'll explore in the chapters ahead, the journey of a space meal doesn't start at the astronaut's plate. It begins years in advance on Earth with careful planning, rigorous testing, and innovative problem-solving. We'll investigate how food is processed, packaged, and preserved for the rigors of space travel. We'll dive into the science behind how our sense of taste changes in space. We'll look at the balancing act of maintaining a healthy diet while contending with limited resources and storage.

Space nutrition also includes the intriguing potential of space agriculture. Could we someday grow our own food beyond Earth's confines? Imagine plucking a ripe tomato from a vine on Mars or crunching into a fresh lettuce leaf grown aboard a spacecraft. These aren't just the dreams of science fiction writers but are active fields of research for scientists and engineers.

As we embark on this journey through the cosmos, examining the fascinating world of "Cosmic Cuisine," we'll uncover how the challenges of space have driven innovation and ingenuity. We'll see that food, far from being a mundane aspect of daily life, becomes a vital lifeline, a piece of home, and a key player in our quest to explore the stars.

Welcome to the table set for the universe. Welcome to the compelling and delicious world of space nutrition.

CHAPTER 2: EARTH TO SPACE: THE EVOLUTION OF ASTRONAUT FOOD

When humans first ventured into the cosmos, they took with them the simplest and most familiar sustenance from their home planet. The food carried by astronauts in the earliest days of space exploration mirrored the era's technology: pragmatic, compact, and innovative, yet rudimentary by today's standards.

Early space food, first developed in the 1960s for NASA's Mercury and Gemini missions, needed to meet several challenging criteria. It had to be lightweight and non-perishable, withstand the forces of launch and the harsh conditions of space, and be easy to eat in a microgravity environment. Most importantly, it had to provide the necessary nutrients to support astronauts in their physically and mentally demanding tasks.

Initial space meals were not particularly appetizing. They resembled baby food more than anything else - a puree of nutrients packed into aluminum tubes. These meals were designed to be squeezed directly into the mouth, a far cry from the traditional dining experience. Yet, they served their purpose, providing the energy and sustenance astronauts needed to perform their duties in space.

As space missions became longer and ventured farther with the Apollo program, the need for more varied and palatable food options became clear. Astronauts needed meals that would not only nourish them but also offer a sense of comfort and normalcy, a psychological salve in the disorienting vastness of space.

The evolution of space food saw the introduction of freeze-dried foods and heat-treated meals, a significant step forward in both taste and texture. By adding water available on the spacecraft, astronauts could rehydrate their meals, providing a more familiar eating experience. These meals, while still a far cry from a home-cooked dinner, offered a broader range of options and better nutrition, contributing significantly to astronauts' well-being.

With the advent of the Space Shuttle program and the International Space Station (ISS), the scope of space cuisine expanded exponentially. More room for storage and advanced systems for heating and rehydrating food allowed for an even greater variety of meals. Astronauts could now enjoy an array of dishes from various cultures, reflecting the international cooperation that characterizes space exploration today.

Importantly, the evolution of astronaut food was also a journey of scientific discovery and technological innovation. It drove developments in food science, packaging, and preservation techniques. The food had to remain safe, nutritious, and somewhat palatable after months - or even years - in storage. The solutions found by researchers not only transformed meals in space but also contributed to food technology on Earth.

As we stand on the precipice of further human space exploration -

with our eyes set on Mars and beyond - the evolution of astronaut food continues. We are moving from a focus on purely sustaining life to enhancing the quality of life. With advancements in space agriculture and ongoing research into more efficient and sustainable food production methods, the future of space cuisine is bound to be fascinating.

In the subsequent chapters of this book, we'll dive deeper into these topics, examining the scientific principles, technological breakthroughs, and human ingenuity that have shaped - and continue to shape - the culinary journey from Earth to space.

CHAPTER 3: THE SCIENCE OF TASTE: HOW ZERO GRAVITY AFFECTS OUR PALATE

How would your favorite dish taste if you were orbiting Earth, gazing upon the swirling blues and whites of our planet, all while floating in the near-weightless environment of a spacecraft? You might imagine the experience to be gastronomically profound, but in reality, the flavors of your meal could be notably altered. Welcome to the science of taste in space.

Several astronauts have reported changes in their sense of taste while in microgravity, noting that foods they usually enjoy seem bland or different in space. This change in perception is not a result of alterations in the food itself but rather a physiological response to the unique conditions of space travel.

Our sense of taste is a complex process that involves multiple sensory inputs beyond the tastebuds on our tongue. Smell plays a critical role, as aromatic molecules released by food enter our nasal passages and interact with olfactory receptors. This combined information from taste and smell gives us the rich perception of flavor that we associate with our favorite foods.

In the microgravity environment of space, however, this process is affected. Without gravity to pull fluids downwards, astronauts often experience a phenomenon similar to congestion, as body fluids shift towards the upper body and head. This fluid shift can cause swelling in nasal tissues, leading to a dulled sense of smell and, consequently, a muted perception of flavor.

To compensate for this muted sense of taste, astronauts often prefer spicier, more strongly flavored foods in space than they do on Earth. Spacecraft kitchens are stocked with a variety of hot sauces, spices, and condiments to help kick up the flavor and make meals more enjoyable.

Apart from flavor, the texture of food also contributes to our eating experience, and here too, space poses challenges. Traditional methods of cooking and preparing food are not feasible due to the lack of gravity and limited resources. Most astronaut foods are dehydrated and require rehydration before eating. While the resulting textures are acceptable, they are not the same as fresh food, and the limited range can lead to meal monotony, further reducing the astronauts' enjoyment of their meals.

Understanding how zero gravity affects taste and the eating experience is important not just for the pleasure of astronauts but also for their health. Ensuring astronauts are motivated to eat their full meals is crucial for providing the energy and nutrients required to maintain their physical health and performance.

Research into the science of taste in space is leading to the development of better food for astronauts, improving not just the nutrition but also the overall dining experience. As we continue our exploration of space, the knowledge gained will be invaluable in ensuring our astronauts remain well-nourished and happy, even millions of miles from their home kitchens.

As we explore in the coming chapters, the challenges of taste in space are just the start of the culinary complexities of astronaut food. From the intricacies of packaging and processing to the potential of space agriculture, there is much more to discover in the world of cosmic cuisine.

CHAPTER 4:
PACKET TO PLATE:
PROCESSING AND
PACKAGING OF
SPACE FOOD

The science behind astronaut food is not just about developing recipes that taste good and provide the necessary nutrients. The real challenge lies in the transformation of these meals from kitchen creations to durable, long-lasting packets that can withstand the harsh conditions of space travel. This chapter will take you on a journey from packet to plate, shedding light on the fascinating world of processing and packaging of space food.

Processing space food requires balancing several considerations. First and foremost, the food must be safe to eat and maintain its nutritional value for an extended period, as it could potentially be stored for months or even years before consumption. It also needs to withstand the physical rigors of space travel, from the violent shaking of the rocket launch to the zero-gravity environment of the International Space Station (ISS) or other spacecraft.

To achieve these goals, two primary methods of food processing are employed: freeze-drying and thermostabilization. Freeze-drying involves freezing the food and then slowly heating it in a vacuum to remove the ice crystals via sublimation, leaving behind a dry and lightweight product. This not only extends the food's shelf life but also significantly reduces its weight, a critical consideration when every ounce of cargo costs thousands of dollars to launch into space.

Thermostabilization, on the other hand, involves heating the food to kill bacteria and other microorganisms, much like the canning process. This method is particularly useful for foods with high water content that do not freeze-dry well. Both methods effectively preserve food without the need for refrigeration, a significant advantage given the energy limitations on spacecraft.

Once the food is processed, the focus shifts to packaging. The packaging needs to be lightweight, compact, and easy to handle in a microgravity environment. It must also protect the food from exposure to the external environment and radiation.

Typically, freeze-dried foods are packaged in vacuum-sealed pouches with a built-in port for the addition of water when it's time to eat. A specially designed galley on the spacecraft is used to inject hot or cold water into the package to rehydrate the food. After a few minutes, the food is ready to be consumed directly from the pouch with a spoon, with the packaging designed to allow easy access while minimizing the chance of crumbs or droplets escaping and floating around in the zero-gravity environment.

Thermostabilized foods, meanwhile, come in flexible retort pouches, a kind of industrial-grade "boil-in-a-bag" product. This packaging is compact, durable, and easy to handle, with a built-in vent that allows for heating in a specialized oven aboard the spacecraft without the risk of the package exploding.

The advancements in space food packaging design are pivotal for the success of long-duration space missions, such as NASA's Artemis Program. These innovations address crucial factors like food safety, reliability, nutrient density, enjoyment, and resource efficiency in a challenging space environment.

Food Safety and Preservation

Advanced packaging technologies are essential for preventing food spoilage and enabling efficient waste processing and recycling. Innovations like Pressure Assisted Thermal Sterilization and Microwave Sterilization enhance the initial quality and nutrition of prepackaged food, extending shelf life up to five years. These technologies ensure food safety, a critical aspect given the absence of traditional cooking methods and the need to minimize resource strain onboard spacecraft.

Resource Efficiency and Reliability

Space food packaging needs to be highly reliable, capable of withstanding harsh conditions, and have a long shelf life while occupying minimal space. Emerging technologies in this area focus on reducing packaging volume and improving the durability of packaging materials to ensure the safety and longevity of food products in space.

Nutrient Density and Enjoyment

Ensuring the palatability and variety of space food is crucial for astronaut morale and health. Innovations like 3D printed food are revolutionizing space cuisine by enabling the creation of diverse, customizable diets. This technology allows for the production of different food designs with specific ingredients, enhancing the eating experience in space.

Closed-Loop Systems and Space Farming

The concept of closed-loop systems in space agriculture is becoming increasingly important. This approach involves using plants not only for food but also for recycling wastewater, generating oxygen, and purifying the air. The Veggie space garden, currently onboard the International Space Station, is an example of a system that can successfully grow various plants in space, contributing to a sustainable living environment.

Real-World Applications

The research and development in space food packaging and production have significant implications for Earth. Technologies like closed-loop greenhouses, vertical farming, and enhanced air purifiers, initially developed for space missions, can be adapted for use in challenging environments on Earth, such as arid regions, polar areas, and densely populated urban centers. Moreover, the ability to produce meat using air components and advanced air purifiers can lead to more sustainable food production methods, reducing the ecological footprint on Earth.

The advancements in space food packaging and production technologies are not only crucial for the success of space missions but also have the potential to revolutionize food production and sustainability on Earth. These innovations represent a significant step forward in our ability to sustain life in space and improve food systems globally.

Through years of research and innovation, food scientists and engineers have refined their techniques to produce foods that are safe, nutritious, and even enjoyable for astronauts. However, challenges remain. The quest for better taste, improved texture, and enhanced nutritional content is ongoing, as is the desire for more sustainable and efficient packaging solutions. As we continue to reach for the stars, the journey from packet to plate promises to be an exciting and evolving aspect of our culinary adventure in space.

CHAPTER 5: MEALTIME AT MACH SPEED: EATING AND DIGESTION IN MICROGRAVITY

With the packaging ripped open and a feast of thermostabilized or rehydrated meals floating before them, astronauts are ready to experience a distinctive feature of life in space: eating in microgravity. The very act of eating, something we take for granted on Earth, becomes a unique and somewhat challenging experience when gravity is taken out of the equation. In this chapter, we dive into the science behind eating and digestion in microgravity and how astronauts manage to maintain their nutrition while navigating these challenges.

In the weightless environment of space, foods don't stay put on plates, and liquids won't remain in cups, leading to an interesting assortment of floating morsels and blobs during meal times. That's why food is typically consumed directly from specially designed pouches. Drinks come in bagged containers with straws that have clamps to prevent the liquid from escaping in zero gravity.

Once the food is safely in an astronaut's mouth, eating isn't too different from what we experience on Earth. Chewing breaks the food down, and saliva begins the chemical digestion process. After swallowing, however, the food embarks on a unique journey.

On Earth, food travels down the esophagus and into the stomach, largely assisted by the force of gravity. But in space, a process called peristalsis becomes even more critical. This is the wave-like muscle contractions of the esophagus that propel food toward the stomach. Even without gravity, peristalsis ensures that food reaches the stomach, where the digestion process continues.

In the stomach, food is churned and mixed with stomach acid to break it down further. But without gravity to help settle the stomach contents, astronauts can experience acid reflux or heartburn more frequently than they would on Earth. Counteracting these issues with medication is part of the standard health regimen for astronauts.

Moving further along the digestive tract, the small intestine absorbs the majority of the nutrients from the food. These nutrients are then circulated throughout the body via the bloodstream, which functions normally in space thanks to the heart's pumping action. However, researchers have found that nutrient absorption might be less efficient in space, potentially due to changes in gut motility or microbiota, though more research is needed.

Once the nutrients are absorbed, the remaining undigested food moves to the large intestine, where water is reabsorbed and the waste compacted. Contrary to what you might think, bowel movements aren't more challenging in space - the muscles involved do their job without the aid of gravity. The real challenge is dealing with the resulting waste in a zero-gravity environment, which we'll explore in detail in a later chapter.

While eating and digestion in space may seem challenging, astronauts adapt quickly to these unique circumstances. Through rigorous training, carefully planned diets, and a pinch of humor, they conquer the difficulties of mealtime at mach speed. As we set our sights on longer space missions, understanding and improving the process of eating and digestion in microgravity will continue to be a critical area of study in the field of space nutrition.

CHAPTER 6: MICRONUTRIENTS AND MACROMOLECULES: BALANCING DIETS IN THE COSMOS

When it comes to nutrition, both on Earth and in space, it all comes down to the delicate balance of micronutrients and macromolecules. These nutritional components are the fuel that drives our bodies, and when we're exploring the stars, they become even more crucial. In this chapter, we'll uncover how space diets are balanced to keep astronauts healthy and productive, the effects of microgravity on nutrient needs, and the future of space nutrition.

Macromolecules include proteins, carbohydrates, and fats – the main sources of energy for our bodies. Proteins are vital for muscle maintenance and growth, something that's of particular importance in a zero-gravity environment where muscle atrophy is a concern. Carbohydrates, on the other hand, provide the primary source of energy for both brain function and physical activities. Lastly, fats, often demonized in diet culture, play a crucial role in nutrient absorption and cell structure.

In space, ensuring a proper balance of these macromolecules in the astronaut's diet is a challenging but critical task. Changes in muscle mass, bone density, and metabolic rates can alter an astronaut's nutritional needs. For instance, to mitigate muscle and bone loss, astronauts may require higher protein intake than the recommended daily amount on Earth. Carbohydrate demands may also fluctuate depending on the intensity and duration of the astronaut's daily physical exercise regimen.

Micronutrients, though needed in much smaller quantities, are equally essential. These include basic vitamins, essential minerals, and trace elements that the body needs to perform a myriad of biochemical functions. For example, Vitamin D, usually synthesized by our body in response to sunlight, is indispensable for calcium absorption and bone health. In the confines of a space station, where exposure to sunlight is non-existent, maintaining sufficient levels of Vitamin D can be a challenge. Similarly, maintaining a balance of minerals like calcium, phosphorus, and potassium is critical to an astronaut's health, given their roles in bone health, energy production, and fluid balance, respectively.

In microgravity, some micronutrient needs may increase. For example, iron is vital for red blood cell production, but in space, where the body produces fewer red blood cells due to plasma volume reduction, the iron requirement is slightly less than on Earth. On the other hand, astronauts may need additional antioxidants, such as vitamins C and E, due to increased oxidative stress in the space environment.

Achieving this delicate nutritional balance is a complex process. It requires an intricate understanding of nutritional science, the effects of space travel on the human body, and the limitations of space food production. Space food must not only provide the necessary nutrients but also be lightweight, long-lasting, and easy to store and prepare.

Future missions, particularly long-duration missions to destinations like Mars, will need to address the challenge of providing a nutritionally balanced diet that can withstand the rigors of space travel. Options could include growing fresh food in space, which would provide additional micronutrients or even potentially biomanufacturing nutrients.

Balancing the diets of astronauts with the right mix of micronutrients and macromolecules is crucial for their health and performance in space. This challenge is amplified by the unique conditions of microgravity, which can significantly alter bodily processes.

Understanding the Balance

Macromolecules

- **Proteins**: Essential for muscle and bone health, especially in microgravity where muscle atrophy and bone density loss are common. Astronauts may require a higher protein intake than on Earth.

- **Carbohydrates**: The primary energy source, crucial for both physical activities and brain functions. The balance of carbohydrate intake must be managed to avoid weight gain due to reduced physical activity in space.

- **Fats**: Important for nutrient absorption and cell structure. The right kind of fats (unsaturated fats) is essential to maintain health without contributing to cardiovascular issues.

Micronutrients

- **Vitamins and Minerals**: Vital for various bodily functions. For example, Vitamin D is crucial for calcium absorption and bone health. In the absence of natural sunlight in space, maintaining sufficient levels of Vitamin D is challenging.

- **Antioxidants**: Space travel increases oxidative stress, making antioxidants like vitamins C and E crucial for protecting cells.

The Challenges in Microgravity

Nutrient Absorption

- Changes in gut motility and microbiota in space can affect how nutrients are absorbed.

- The fluid shift towards the upper body can impact the absorption and processing of nutrients.

Nutritional Strategies for Space

Personalized Nutrition

- Tailoring diets to individual astronaut's needs, considering their health, activity level, and specific challenges they face in microgravity.

Food Variety

- A varied diet ensures a wide range of nutrients are consumed, preventing deficiencies.

Future Perspectives

- As space missions get longer, understanding and adapting these nutritional strategies will be key.
- Research into how microgravity affects nutrient absorption and metabolism is ongoing, which will inform future dietary guidelines for astronauts.

Balancing the diets of astronauts with the right mix of macromolecules and micronutrients is a complex yet vital task. It requires a thorough understanding of nutritional science, the effects of space travel on the human body, and the limitations of space food systems. This balance is not just crucial for physical health but also for mental well-being, making it a cornerstone of successful space missions.

As we continue to explore the cosmos, the field of space nutrition will play an ever-increasing role in astronaut health and mission success. By understanding and meeting the nutritional demands of astronauts in space, we not only increase our ability to venture deeper into the universe but also gain valuable insights into human health and nutrition that can be applied back here on Earth.

CHAPTER 7: INTERSTELLAR HYDRATION: THE CHALLENGE OF WATER IN SPACE

Water – it's one of the most basic elements of life as we know it. On Earth, it's readily available, but in space, the story is completely different. It's heavy, difficult to store, and every drop is precious. This chapter delves into the unique challenges and creative solutions for managing water in the void, from quenching astronauts' thirst to growing plants for food.

Water is not just essential for hydration; it also plays a critical role in food rehydration, hygiene, and cooling systems on spacecraft. Therefore, one of the primary goals of any space mission is minimizing the amount of water needed to be carried from Earth and maximizing the efficiency of its use.

One innovative solution to this problem has been the development of water recovery systems that recycle virtually every drop of water on board a spacecraft. These systems are designed to capture and filter moisture from every possible source. Sweat, urine, and even the humidity in the astronauts' breath are collected, filtered, and processed back into drinkable water. It's an impressive if somewhat distasteful, example of how necessity drives innovation.

Even with the recycling of water, though, the supply is not unlimited. As such, the water content in astronaut food must be considered. Traditionally, space food has been dehydrated to reduce weight and extend shelf life. While effective, this approach requires a significant amount of water for rehydration before consumption. As we move towards longer-duration missions, new food preparation technologies that minimize the need for water are under investigation, such as high-pressure thermal sterilization and microwave sterilization.

Hydration in space also presents a unique challenge for the human body. Fluid distribution changes in microgravity, leading to a phenomenon astronauts call "puffy face, bird legs" syndrome. Fluids move toward the upper body, making astronauts feel like they have a constant cold. Although it doesn't pose a serious health risk, it can be uncomfortable and affect the body's perception of hydration.

Additionally, water's role extends beyond quenching thirst and preparing food. It's also crucial for space agriculture, another component of long-duration space missions. As we look towards growing food in space, we face the challenge of how to water plants in a weightless environment. Methods such as hydroponics and aeroponics, which use significantly less water than traditional farming, are currently being studied for their potential use in space agriculture.

The search for water also guides the exploration of our solar system. Places like Mars and the moon's poles, where water ice has been detected, have become high-priority targets for future manned missions and potential off-world colonization. After all, where there's water, there's the potential for life – or at least, the ability to sustain it.

In short, water is a vital resource for life, and in space, its management poses unique challenges. Understanding and overcoming these challenges is crucial for long-duration space missions and future space habitats.

Water in Space: Essential and Scarce

- **Critical for Hydration**: In space, ensuring adequate hydration is vital due to altered fluid distribution in microgravity.

- **Food Preparation**: Water is essential for rehydrating freeze-dried space foods.

- **Hygiene and Cooling Systems**: Water plays a crucial role in maintaining hygiene and cooling systems aboard spacecraft.

Water Recycling: A Necessity in Space

- **Closed-Loop Systems**: Space missions use advanced recycling systems to purify and reuse water from various sources, including humidity, sweat, and urine.

- **Efficiency and Sustainability**: These systems aim for maximal water recovery to reduce the need for resupply from Earth, crucial for sustainability.

Challenges and Innovations

- **Fluid Distribution in Microgravity**: Managing water in a weightless environment is complex, with issues like water blob formation and distribution.

- **Space Agriculture**: Watering plants in space requires innovative techniques like hydroponics and aeroponics, which use less water and no soil.

Water on Moon and Mars Missions

- **In-Situ Resource Utilization**: Future missions to the Moon and Mars plan to utilize local resources, such as extracting water ice from lunar poles or Martian soil.

- **Sustainable Habitats**: Creating self-sustaining habitats on these celestial bodies hinges on effective water management.

Earth Benefits

- **Technological Innovations**: Space water recycling technologies can benefit Earth, particularly in areas with limited water resources.

Managing water in space involves a multifaceted approach, addressing the challenges of microgravity, recycling, and sustainability. These efforts not only support life in space but also hold potential applications for improving water management on Earth.

In conclusion, the interstellar journey isn't just about reaching new galaxies; it's also about understanding and adapting to the fundamental constraints of life-supporting resources. As we continue to explore the cosmos, learning to efficiently manage, recycle, and appreciate our water sources will be essential, teaching us valuable lessons not only for space exploration but also for the preservation and conservation of our resources here on Earth.

CHAPTER 8: GROWING GREENS IN THE GALAXY: THE BASICS OF SPACE AGRICULTURE

As we've delved into the complexities of space food, we've discussed how it's prepared, packaged, and consumed. However, for long-duration missions or potential colonization efforts, relying solely on food brought from Earth isn't feasible. Enter space agriculture, an emerging field focusing on the challenge of cultivating crops beyond Earth's atmosphere.

Space agriculture's core goal is to create sustainable, self-sufficient food production systems that can support life in extraterrestrial environments. These efforts extend beyond just feeding astronauts. Plants also contribute to life-support systems by recycling carbon dioxide into breathable oxygen and assisting in water purification, making space agriculture a pivotal player in the broader concept of bioregenerative life-support systems.

In the unique environment of space, however, traditional farming methods don't apply. Gravity, or the lack thereof, changes everything, from how water and nutrients are distributed to how plants orient themselves. Consequently, traditional soil-based cultivation is impractical, driving scientists to explore alternatives like hydroponics and aeroponics.

Early experiments with space gardening have predominantly involved small, fast-growing, and leafy plants like lettuce, radishes, or mustard greens. The first-ever space-grown lettuce, eaten by astronauts aboard the orbiting International Space Station (ISS) in 2015, was a milestone moment in space agriculture. The lettuce was grown using a system known as "Veggie," which utilized LED lights to stimulate plant growth.

But leafy greens alone won't sustain a space-faring population. Future research aims to broaden the cosmic menu with investigations into growing a wider variety of crops, including fruiting plants like tomatoes and peppers. Understanding how these plants reproduce, grow, and mature in a microgravity environment is an ongoing research focus.

Genetic engineering also offers promising avenues for future space agriculture. Scientists are exploring how to modify plants to thrive in the unique conditions of space, with desired traits including more efficient nutrient uptake, faster growth rates, and even the ability to withstand potential extraterrestrial pathogens.

In terms of practicality, space agriculture faces significant constraints regarding available space and resources. Therefore, systems need to be compact, energy-efficient, and virtually closed to prevent waste. Achieving high crop yield in a small area without access to natural sunlight presents ongoing challenges.

Moreover, farming in space is not just about food and life support.

It also holds psychological benefits. The act of tending plants can provide astronauts with a connection to nature, offering a much-needed mental break from the harsh realities of living in space.

The advent of space agriculture marks a revolutionary step in human space exploration, extending our ability to cultivate crops beyond Earth's atmosphere.

Core Objective

Space agriculture aims to create sustainable, self-sufficient food production systems in space. It's not just about feeding astronauts; it also contributes to life-support systems by recycling carbon dioxide into oxygen and purifying water, making it a crucial element in bioregenerative life-support systems.

Farming Methods in Space

Traditional soil-based cultivation is impractical in space. Thus, alternative methods like hydroponics (growing plants in nutrient-rich water) and aeroponics (where plants are suspended in air and misted with nutrients) are being explored.

Early Space Gardening Experiments

Small, fast-growing, leafy plants like lettuce and radishes have been successfully grown in space environments, such as aboard the International Space Station (ISS). These initial experiments are pivotal in understanding how plants grow and develop in space.

Genetic Engineering and Crop Improvement

Biotechnological advancements are playing a significant role in space agriculture. Genetic engineering can be utilized to develop plants that are more suited to the unique conditions of space, such as enhanced nutrient uptake or resistance to extraterrestrial pathogens.

Sustainability and Resource Constraints

Space agriculture systems need to be compact, efficient, and almost entirely closed to prevent waste. Achieving high crop yields in a confined space without natural sunlight and with limited resources is one of the major challenges.

Psychological Benefits

Beyond nutritional value, space agriculture offers psychological benefits for astronauts. Tending to plants can provide a connection to Earth and a welcome diversion from the confines of space habitats.

While still in its infancy, space agriculture is a field brimming with potential, driven by the need to nourish our ambition to venture further into the cosmos. As we sow the seeds of interstellar cultivation, we take one step closer to turning the dream of long-duration space travel into a reality.

Space agriculture is essential for the future of space exploration. Its development not only supports the goal of extended human presence in space but also provides insights into sustainable agricultural practices on Earth. As we continue to innovate and experiment, the dream of self-sustaining space habitats with thriving space farms becomes increasingly tangible.

CHAPTER 9: ASTROPONICS: THE SCIENCE OF HYDROPONICS AND AEROPONICS IN SPACE

As we move from terrestrial farming towards growing plants in the vacuum of space, conventional methods of cultivation quickly prove inadequate. Enter astroponics, the novel blend of hydroponics and aeroponics adapted to the peculiarities of life beyond Earth's atmosphere. In this chapter, we explore the principles and practices that drive these two distinct yet complementary systems and how they might facilitate sustainable agriculture in space.

The concept of hydroponics involves growing plants in a nutrient-rich water solution instead of soil. Without the need for traditional soil, hydroponics offers a clean, efficient, and surprisingly space-effective method of cultivation, with advantages that include better control over nutrient delivery and no reliance on natural rainfall or fertile land.

However, hydroponics faces unique challenges in a microgravity environment. In space, water behaves differently, forming spherical globules instead of flowing downward due to gravitational pull. Thus, delivering a steady supply of nutrient-infused water without drowning the plants—or letting them dry out—requires novel systems.

One such solution is the use of specially designed root mats, which keep the plant roots moist without causing waterlogging. These hydroponic systems, such as the Vegetable Production System (Veggie) used aboard the ISS, use LED lights to provide the necessary spectrum of light for photosynthesis and have successfully grown a variety of leafy greens in space.

On the other hand, aeroponics represents an even more radical departure from traditional farming. In aeroponic systems, plants are suspended in air, and their roots are periodically misted with nutrient-rich water. This technique eliminates the need for soil and even water reservoirs necessary in hydroponics, offering a remarkably resource-efficient method for food production in space.

NASA has shown a keen interest in aeroponic technology. Its benefits, including faster plant growth, greater plant density, and efficient use of water and nutrients, make it particularly suited to the resource-limited environment of space. However, just like hydroponics, aeroponics faces the challenge of water and nutrient delivery in microgravity. Innovative solutions, such as the use of misting nozzles and porous materials to deliver nutrients, are under active research.

Yet, the success of astroponics hinges on more than just nutrient delivery. Factors such as lighting, temperature, humidity, carbon dioxide levels, and potential microbial contamination all require careful monitoring and control. Moreover, it's crucial to consider the human element: ensuring the system is user-friendly for astronauts who are scientists and explorers, not typically trained as farmers.

Hydroponics in Space

- **Concept**: Growing plants in a nutrient-rich water solution, eliminating the need for soil.
- **Microgravity Challenges**: Adapting hydroponic systems to function effectively in the absence of gravity.
- **Advancements**: Development of root mats and specialized systems for nutrient delivery in microgravity.

Aeroponics: A Step Further

- **Method**: Suspending plants in air and misting their roots with nutrients.
- **Advantages**: Minimizes water and nutrient use, offering a highly efficient method for food production in space.
- **Challenges**: Ensuring consistent nutrient delivery and plant support in a zero-gravity environment.

Plant Growth and Development

- **Role of Microbiomes**: Understanding and leveraging plant-associated microbial communities is crucial for robust plant growth in space.
- **Genetic Engineering**: Customizing probiotic supplements and manipulating plant genetics to thrive in space conditions.

Sustainability and Efficiency

- **Resource Utilization**: Astroponic systems aim for maximum resource efficiency, reducing the need for water and nutrients.

- **Self-Sustaining Systems**: Integrating astroponics into life support systems for oxygen production and carbon dioxide absorption.

Future Prospects

- **Research and Development**: Ongoing studies to optimize these systems for wider crop variety and improved efficiency.

- **Implications for Earth**: Innovations in astroponics can be applied to improve agricultural practices in extreme environments on Earth.

Astroponics represents a vital component of future space missions, offering a sustainable and efficient solution for food production in the cosmos. Its development will not only advance our space exploration capabilities but also has the potential to enhance agricultural practices on Earth, particularly in resource-constrained environments.

Despite the challenges, astroponics promises a tantalizing vision of the future: a spaceship, or even a Mars base, teeming with lush, green growth chambers, providing fresh food, recycling waste, and improving astronauts' psychological well-being. It's a bold vision that draws us one step closer to self-sustaining life in space. As we deepen our understanding of astroponics, we sow the seeds for tomorrow's cosmic cuisine.

CHAPTER 10: LUNAR FARMING: THE POTENTIAL FOR AGRICULTURE ON THE MOON

The Moon, our closest celestial neighbor, has captivated the human imagination for millennia. As space agencies and private entities set their sights on the lunar surface, the concept of lunar farming—the cultivation of crops on the Moon—has evolved from science fiction into a topic of serious scientific investigation. This chapter explores the potential and the challenges of lunar agriculture, a cornerstone for the vision of a self-sustaining lunar base.

The environment of the Moon poses significant challenges to traditional methods of agriculture. With no atmosphere, extreme temperature fluctuations, a fourteen-day night, and regolith devoid of organic matter, farming on the Moon may seem insurmountable. However, with innovative technologies and a touch of terrestrial ingenuity, scientists are exploring the potential for lunar agriculture.

One key strategy involves the use of controlled, closed environments—essentially, greenhouses on the Moon. These structures would need to carefully regulate temperature, humidity, light, and carbon dioxide levels to mimic Earth-like conditions for plant growth. Advanced systems such as hydroponics or aeroponics, discussed in Chapter 9, offer potential solutions for soilless cultivation in these environments.

Scientists are also exploring the potential of lunar regolith, the layer of loose, fragmented material covering solid bedrock, as a medium for plant growth. While the lunar regolith lacks the organic nutrients found in Earth's soil, it contains many essential mineral elements like silicon, aluminum, and iron. With the addition of missing nutrients and potential microbial partners, this lifeless dust could potentially support plant life. Experiments like NASA's Lunar Plant Growth Habitat project aim to test this hypothesis.

However, to farm the lunar surface sustainably, we must also address the issue of resources. Water, a crucial ingredient for life and agriculture, is scarce on the Moon. Recent discoveries of water ice in permanently shadowed craters near the lunar poles offer some hope, but extracting this water presents its own challenges. Efficient recycling of water and nutrients within the closed-environment systems will be essential for sustainable lunar farming.

Energy is another significant challenge. Sunlight, the driving force behind photosynthesis, is absent half the time on the Moon due to its lengthy lunar night. Relying on artificial light would require large amounts of power, a precious resource on the Moon. Innovative solutions, such as genetically modified plants that can withstand long periods of darkness or energy-efficient lighting systems, could potentially help overcome this challenge.

The idea of lunar farming also raises interesting questions about what crops to grow. Nutrient-dense, fast-growing, and low-maintenance plants would likely be the best candidates. It's also important to consider the psychological value of crops; fresh, flavorful food can provide a significant morale boost to lunar inhabitants far from home.

Unique Challenges of the Lunar Environment

- **Extreme Conditions**: The Moon's lack of atmosphere, extreme temperature variations, and long lunar nights present significant obstacles.
- **Soil Quality**: Lunar regolith lacks organic nutrients, necessitating innovative approaches to create a viable growth medium.

Controlled Environment Agriculture

- **Greenhouse Solutions**: Controlled environments with regulated temperature, light, and humidity are essential for lunar farming.
- **Hydroponics and Aeroponics**: Soilless cultivation methods are promising for growing plants in lunar habitats.

Water Resource Management

- **Utilizing Lunar Water Ice**: Extracting and purifying water from the lunar poles is key to sustainable farming on the Moon.

- **Efficient Water Recycling**: Closed-loop systems for water conservation are crucial due to the scarcity of water resources.

Energy and Light Management

- **Solar Energy Utilization**: Harnessing solar energy during the long lunar day and finding solutions for the lunar night are vital.
- **Artificial Lighting**: Developing energy-efficient lighting systems for plant growth during the lunar night.

Crop Selection and Genetic Engineering

- **Suitable Crops**: Focus on nutrient-dense, fast-growing crops that require minimal maintenance.
- **Genetic Modifications**: Potential for genetically modified crops to thrive in the harsh lunar environment.

Lunar farming represents a blend of science, technology, and innovation, essential for establishing a sustainable human presence on the Moon. Overcoming the numerous challenges will not only pave the way for lunar colonization but also offer insights into improving agriculture in extreme environments on Earth. As we advance our lunar explorations, the dream of cultivating crops on the Moon becomes an exciting and tangible reality.

In summary, while lunar farming faces many challenges, its potential benefits make it a worthwhile endeavor. The knowledge and technologies developed could not only pave the way for sustained human presence on the Moon but also offer insights to tackle agricultural challenges on Earth. As we forge ahead into this uncharted territory, the dream of seeing green shoots sprouting against the grayscale lunar landscape becomes ever more vivid.

CHAPTER 11:
MARTIAN HARVEST:
CHALLENGES AND
OPPORTUNITIES FOR
FARMING ON MARS

As space exploration extends towards the fourth planet from the Sun, the question of sustainable life on Mars has risen to prominence. In order to establish a long-term human presence on Mars, reliable and sustainable food production is essential. This chapter delves into the formidable challenges and unprecedented opportunities that await the pioneers of Martian farming.

Mars offers a host of obstacles for traditional agriculture. It has a thin and predominantly carbon dioxide atmosphere, a cold and dry environment, and a soil—referred to as Martian regolith—that contains toxic perchlorate salts. Furthermore, while the Martian day is roughly equivalent to an Earth day, its sunlight is only about half as intense, which could hinder photosynthesis.

However, through these challenges shine several opportunities for revolutionary advances in agricultural science. Similar to lunar farming strategies, Martian agriculture will rely heavily on controlled environments such as greenhouses. These structures would have to create Earth-like conditions for crops, including ideal temperature, light, humidity, and nutrient availability. They'd also need to offer protection from the high levels of cosmic radiation that Mars' thin atmosphere fails to block.

Addressing the issue of Martian soil toxicity, researchers are investigating the potential use of certain microorganisms to break down the harmful perchlorate salts in the soil, making it safe for plant growth. This bio-remediation process, if successful, could dramatically transform the prospects for Mars agriculture.

Hydroponic and aeroponic systems, covered in Chapter 9, are also excellent candidates for Martian agriculture. These soilless cultivation methods, combined with careful water and nutrient recycling, could minimize resource usage—an essential factor when considering the cost of transporting materials to Mars.

As for the selection of crops, leafy greens, legumes, and certain fruits are likely candidates due to their nutrient density, relatively short growth periods, and minimum maintenance needs. Future missions could also consider mushrooms, as certain fungi can break down dead plant matter, aiding nutrient recycling.

The use of genetically modified organisms (GMOs) could also play a critical role. GMOs could be engineered for hardiness in the Martian environment, increased nutrient content, or even the ability to utilize the abundant carbon dioxide in the Martian atmosphere for photosynthesis, similar to certain cyanobacteria on Earth.

Excitingly, the question of water, a critical resource for agriculture, received an optimistic answer when the Mars

Reconnaissance Orbiter discovered evidence of liquid water flowing intermittently on the planet's surface. While the extraction and purification of this water present logistical challenges, this discovery fuels hope for sustainable agriculture on Mars.

Martian Environment: Harsh and Unforgiving

- **Soil and Atmosphere**: Martian regolith contains toxic perchlorate salts, and the atmosphere is thin, primarily composed of carbon dioxide.
- **Temperature and Sunlight**: Mars experiences extreme cold, and its sunlight is less intense than Earth's, affecting photosynthesis.

Technological Innovations for Martian Farming

- **Controlled Environments**: Development of greenhouses to create Earth-like conditions, including temperature, humidity, and light control.
- **Hydroponics and Aeroponics**: Soilless cultivation methods are essential due to the lack of organic soil on Mars.

Water and Nutrient Management

- **Water Extraction and Recycling**: Utilizing Martian water resources, such as sub-surface ice, and recycling water within closed-loop systems.
- **Nutrient Delivery**: Innovations in nutrient delivery systems adapted for Martian conditions.

Genetic Engineering and Crop Selection

- **Crop Adaptation**: Engineering crops to withstand Martian conditions, focusing on hardiness, nutrient content, and efficient growth.
- **Diverse Crops**: Exploring the growth of a variety of plants, from leafy greens to fruiting crops, to ensure a balanced diet.

Sustainability and Long-Term Viability

- **Resource Efficiency**: Maximizing resource use efficiency, including water, nutrients, and energy.
- **Sustainable Habitats**: Integrating agriculture into Martian habitats for self-sufficiency and life support.

Ethical and Ecological Considerations

- **Responsible Exploration**: Addressing ethical considerations in altering a planetary ecosystem.
- **Environmental Impact**: Assessing and minimizing the ecological footprint of Martian farming practices.

Farming on Mars presents a unique set of challenges and opportunities, requiring innovative solutions and careful planning.

In summary, while the Martian environment poses significant challenges, the convergence of multiple scientific disciplines —biology, botany, geology, and engineering—offers innovative solutions for Martian agriculture. The potential to harvest on

Mars not only takes us one step closer to a self-sustaining colony on the Red Planet but also provides valuable insights to improve agricultural practices here on Earth, fostering a truly interplanetary exchange of knowledge.

CHAPTER 12: THE ROLE OF GENETICALLY ENGINEERED CROPS IN SPACE AGRICULTURE

The cultivation of genetically engineered (GE) crops could play a critical role in the success of space agriculture. These crops, engineered for specific traits, could provide an essential means of adapting plants to the unique challenges of space environments. This chapter delves into the role and potential of these technological marvels in sustaining life beyond our home planet.

Genetic engineering offers us a toolkit for redesigning crops in ways that could make them more suitable for space cultivation. This might involve enhancing their nutritional content, improving their efficiency in resource utilization, increasing their resistance to environmental stress, or even enabling them to perform new functions, such as the extraction of harmful compounds from the environment.

To confront the lower light conditions in places like Mars, scientists could engineer crops to perform photosynthesis more efficiently. This might involve modifying plants to absorb and use a broader spectrum of light or to use the available light more effectively. Also, crops might be engineered to withstand the high levels of radiation in space, enhancing their survival and productivity.

One key area of genetic engineering that holds promise for space agriculture is the creation of crops that require fewer resources. For example, crops could be designed to grow optimally in hydroponic or aeroponic systems, thereby requiring less water and no soil. Similarly, they could be engineered to require fewer nutrients, making them easier to grow in nutrient-limited conditions.

One of the most exciting prospects of genetic engineering in space agriculture is the possibility of engineering crops to perform functions that go beyond providing food. This might involve creating plants that can purify the air by removing harmful substances or even generating oxygen. Some scientists are exploring the concept of "biological life support systems" in which plants play a crucial role in maintaining the atmospheric balance within space habitats.

The development of GE crops for space also raises several ethical and regulatory considerations. Genetically engineered organisms need to be controlled and monitored to prevent unintended consequences, such as the creation of new pathogens or the disruption of ecosystems, should they escape into the environment. This requires robust biocontainment strategies, as well as careful risk assessment and management.

Nevertheless, the development of genetically engineered (GE) crops holds significant potential for space agriculture, offering customized solutions to the challenges of growing food in extraterrestrial environments.

Advantages of Genetic Engineering

- **Enhanced Nutritional Content**: Genetic modifications can boost the nutritional value of crops, vital for astronaut health.

- **Resource Utilization**: Engineering crops to grow in hydroponic or aeroponic systems can reduce the need for water and soil.

- **Stress Tolerance**: Modifying plants to withstand the extreme conditions of space, such as radiation and microgravity.

Ethical and Safety Considerations

- **Biocontainment**: Ensuring genetically modified organisms do not adversely affect space environments or, upon return, Earth's ecosystems.

- **Regulatory Compliance**: Adhering to international standards and ethical guidelines in the modification and use of GE crops.

Future Directions

- **Biological Life Support Systems**: Exploring the potential of GE crops to contribute to life support systems, including air purification and waste recycling.

- **Interdisciplinary Collaboration**: Combining insights from genetics, space science, and agriculture to advance GE crop development for space use.

Genetically engineered crops offer innovative solutions to the challenges of space agriculture, enhancing the possibility of sustainable life in space. Ethical and regulatory considerations are crucial in this endeavor, ensuring that these advancements benefit both space exploration and Earth-based agriculture.

The exploration of genetically engineered crops for space farming is still in its early stages, with much research and testing needed. Yet the potential of this technology is immense. By tweaking the genetic code of our crops, we might not only be able to grow food in the hostile environments of other planets but also create crops that could support the overall sustainability of life in space. This research is not only critical for our future in the cosmos but also holds great promise for improving agriculture and food security here on Earth.

CHAPTER 13:
COMPOSTING IN THE COSMOS: WASTE MANAGEMENT AND SUSTAINABILITY IN SPACE

As we inch closer to long-term space missions and extraterrestrial colonies, sustainability becomes a primary concern. Our current model of waste disposal on Earth is unsustainable in space. One strategy for addressing this problem is through composting, a natural process that converts organic waste materials into nutrient-rich soil. This chapter explores the science, challenges, and potential solutions for composting in the cosmos.

The concept of composting in space isn't just about waste disposal; it's also about resource reutilization. On long-term space missions or planetary colonies, we'll need to recycle as much as possible. This includes organic waste – from both plant and human sources. Composting could provide a means to convert this waste into a valuable resource: nutrient-rich soil for space agriculture.

Composting is a biological process driven by microorganisms that slowly break down organic matter into simpler compounds. This process requires the right balance of carbon-rich materials (like plant matter), nitrogen-rich materials (like food scraps), water, and oxygen. The microgravity environment of space presents some unique challenges to achieving this balance. For example, maintaining adequate aeration (oxygen supply) for the composting microorganisms can be difficult in a microgravity environment.

However, scientists are developing solutions to these challenges. One approach is to use specialized composting reactors designed to work in a microgravity environment. These reactors could use mechanical or fluidic systems to ensure adequate aeration and mixing of the composting materials. Another approach might involve the use of specific microbial strains selected or engineered for their ability to compost effectively in microgravity.

Furthermore, composting could play a role in broader waste management and life support systems in space. For example, the heat generated by the composting process could be harnessed for energy. The carbon dioxide produced by the composting microorganisms could be captured and fed into plant growth systems, contributing to the carbon cycle in a closed-loop life support system.

Of course, there are many safety considerations when composting in space. These include the prevention of pathogen growth, the containment of composting processes to avoid contamination of the spacecraft environment, and the handling and processing of human waste.

Composting in the cosmos represents a unique intersection of biology, engineering, and space science. It's a field that is still very much in its infancy but one that holds significant promise for the future of space travel and colonization. By developing effective and safe methods for composting in space, we can take a significant step towards sustainable living beyond Earth.

CHAPTER 14: FUTURE FEASTS: THE NEW FRONTIERS OF SPACE FOOD TECHNOLOGY

As we continue our exploration of space, the food we bring with us will play an increasingly critical role. With missions getting longer, our ability to provide astronauts with nutritious, appealing, and long-lasting food is essential. The future of space food technology will not just be about sustenance; it will be about maximizing health, morale, and performance in an environment that is fundamentally different from Earth.

Future space food technology could involve several advancements. For one, we can expect to see improvements in the processing and packaging of space food. While today's space food is already a far cry from the "squeeze tubes" of the early space age, further advancements could lead to even greater variety, quality, and convenience. For example, developments in preservation techniques could extend the shelf life of foods without sacrificing taste or nutritional value. This will be particularly important for long-duration missions to Mars or beyond.

Furthermore, as we continue to learn about the unique nutritional needs of astronauts in microgravity, we can expect future space food to be more personalized. Precision nutrition – tailoring an individual's diet to their specific needs based on their genetics, metabolism, and other factors – is a growing field on Earth, and it's likely to have applications in space as well.

Advancements in space agriculture will also play a key role in the future of space food technology. As we've explored in previous chapters, growing crops in space can provide fresh food, contribute to life support systems, and even have psychological benefits for astronauts. Advances in space farming technologies could lead to the production of a wider diversity of crops, improving the diversity and quality of space diets.

Another potential frontier in space food technology is the use of alternative protein sources, such as cultured meat or insects. Cultured meat, also referred to as lab-grown meat, is manufactured by culturing animal cells in a lab, a process that could potentially be adapted for space. Insects, on the other hand, are highly efficient at converting feed into protein, require relatively little space, and could also serve as a way to recycle organic waste.

Lastly, advances in additive manufacturing, also known as 3D printing, could revolutionize space food preparation. Rather than bringing a variety of foods from Earth, astronauts could bring a set of basic ingredients and print their meals on demand. This could allow for unprecedented variety and customization in astronauts' diets while reducing the weight and volume of food supplies.

The future of space food technology holds exciting possibilities that will not only keep astronauts fed but also contribute to their health, performance, and morale on long-duration missions. As we continue to reach for the stars, our approach to feeding astronauts will continue to evolve, driven by advances in science and technology.

CHAPTER 15: SPACE CUISINE AND CULTURAL CONSIDERATIONS: FOOD FOR A MULTI-NATIONAL CREW

When considering the nutritional needs of astronauts, we must also account for cultural and personal preferences. Space agencies from around the world contribute to a multicultural crew on international space stations and missions, each bringing their unique culinary heritage. How does one cater to a diverse palate while providing the necessary nutrition and ensuring the food's suitability for space travel? This chapter delves into the intersection of space cuisine and cultural considerations.

Food is more than just sustenance—it's a reflection of our culture, our history, and our identity. It offers comfort, sparks memories, and fosters a sense of community. In the confines of a spacecraft or space station, these aspects become even more important. Food can serve as a psychological support, reinforcing an astronaut's connection to home and their cultural identity while providing variety and enjoyment in an otherwise monotonous environment.

NASA, ESA, Roscosmos, and other international space agencies have long recognized this and have taken steps to include a variety of foods in their space menus, reflecting the diverse backgrounds of their astronauts. For example, NASA's food lab has worked with its international counterparts to develop space-friendly versions of a variety of international dishes, from American shrimp cocktail and Russian borscht to Japanese sushi and Italian espresso. Each astronaut is also allowed to bring a small quantity of "bonus foods" of their choosing, which often includes favorite snacks or comfort foods from home.

However, developing these culturally diverse menus is not without challenges. Each dish must meet the strict criteria for space food: it must be nutritionally balanced, long-lasting, and able to withstand the rigors of space travel. It must also be easy to eat in microgravity and produce minimal waste.

To meet these requirements, space agencies use various food processing techniques, including dehydration, heat treatment, and irradiation, to ensure safety and long shelf-life. In addition, dishes must often be adapted to meet these constraints. For instance, foods that are crumbly or sticky can pose a hazard in microgravity and are thus unsuitable for space travel in their original form.

Moreover, culinary preferences can vary widely among a multicultural crew. Spices and flavorings that are enjoyable to some may be off-putting to others. Balancing these preferences while ensuring a variety of options is a careful act.

The development of space agriculture, as we have discussed in earlier chapters, could also play a role in enabling more culturally diverse cuisine in space. As the ability to grow a wider range of crops in space improves, astronauts may eventually be able to cook fresh meals using a variety of ingredients, enabling more culinary creativity and cultural expression.

Catering to the cultural and personal preferences of astronauts is not just a matter of morale—it also plays a role in nutrition. Research has shown that astronauts tend to consume less food in space than on Earth, which can cause problematic weight loss and nutritional deficiencies. Providing astronauts with a variety of enjoyable and culturally relevant foods can help combat this issue by encouraging them to eat more.

As we continue to explore the cosmos, food will remain a crucial component of space travel—not just for survival but for the well-being and morale of our astronauts. Catering to a diverse crew's culinary tastes and preferences, in addition to their nutritional needs, will be an essential aspect of future space missions.

CHAPTER 16: THE PSYCHOLOGICAL IMPACT OF FOOD IN SPACE: COMFORT AND MORALE IN THE VOID

As we venture deeper into space, the psychological well-being of astronauts becomes as crucial as their physical health. In the confines of a spacecraft or a space station, food serves more than just a biological necessity. It is a source of comfort, a tether to home, a diversion from the repetitive environment, and a fundamental aspect of crew morale. This chapter delves into the role of food in maintaining mental health and cohesion among astronauts during space missions.

In an environment as extreme and foreign as space, familiar routines and pleasures become invaluable. The act of eating, a ritual as old as humankind, becomes an anchor of normalcy. Beyond that, the taste, smell, and texture of food can serve as powerful reminders of home, offering psychological comfort. From enjoying a favorite dish to celebrating a holiday with a special meal, these experiences help astronauts feel connected to their lives on Earth.

In addition, food plays a significant role in the social dynamics of a space crew. Shared meals are a time for relaxation, camaraderie, and informal communication. It is during these moments that astronauts can step back from their technical roles and engage as a social unit. As such, the dining area is often considered the heart of the spacecraft, fostering a sense of community in the isolated environment of space.

However, eating in space is not without its challenges. As previously discussed, the microgravity environment alters the perception of taste, which can lead to a decreased enjoyment of food. Combined with the constraints of space food processing, this can result in a limited and monotonous diet. Over time, this can contribute to "menu fatigue," where astronauts grow tired of eating the same foods and start consuming less than their required intake. This phenomenon is a concern not only for physical health but also for mental well-being, as enjoyment of food is tied to overall morale.

Space agencies have made considerable efforts to combat menu fatigue by offering a wide variety of foods and allowing astronauts to select their preferred meals before the mission. The option to grow and harvest fresh produce in space, as explored in previous chapters, also adds diversity and offers a gratifying, hands-on activity that can boost morale.

The potential for psychological support is another factor taken into account when designing space menus. "Comfort foods" that hold particular sentimental value for astronauts, such as holiday treats or favorite snacks, may also hold a profound influence on individual mood and morale. Acknowledging cultural diversity, as we discussed in the previous chapter, is also important in catering to the comfort and preferences of a multi-national crew.

Looking toward future long-duration missions, such as those to Mars, the psychological impact of food becomes even more critical. The isolation, extreme environment, and distance from Earth will pose considerable mental health challenges, and food will be a vital tool in addressing these issues.

As we advance our exploration of the cosmos, understanding the complex role of food in space is essential. It is not just about nourishing the body but also about feeding the spirit, providing comfort, and fostering unity in the void. This perspective will be critical in designing future food systems for space travel, ensuring that they provide for both the nutritional and psychological needs of astronauts.

CHAPTER 17: FROM ASTRO-FOOD TO EARTH: APPLICATIONS OF SPACE FOOD RESEARCH ON EARTH

Though born out of necessity for sustaining life in the extreme conditions of space, the research and advancements made in astronaut food and space agriculture bear significant implications for our lives on Earth. In this chapter, we'll delve into how these innovations have trickled down to improve terrestrial food systems, agriculture, sustainability practices, and even disaster management.

One of the primary challenges in developing space food has been the creation of nutritionally balanced meals with a long shelf life that remain appealing to the palate. The technologies developed to address these needs, such as freeze-drying and thermostabilization, have found widespread use in the creation of emergency rations and humanitarian aid supplies. These meals, like their space counterparts, must be lightweight, easy to transport, and capable of withstanding varying conditions while maintaining their nutritional value.

In our quest to develop space agriculture, we've pioneered methods for growing crops with minimal resources, using hydroponics and aeroponics systems that require no soil and significantly less water than traditional farming methods. These techniques have potential applications in urban farming, where space is limited, and in regions with arid conditions or poor soil quality.

The closed-loop systems designed for long-duration space missions, which incorporate plant growth not just for food but also for oxygen production and carbon dioxide absorption, have sparked interest in Earth-based sustainability efforts. Earth's ecosystems, after all, are closed-loop systems on a larger scale. Lessons from space agriculture could inform our approach to managing Earth's resources more efficiently, potentially aiding in our response to climate change.

The recycling and waste management strategies explored in space, such as composting and waste-to-resource technologies, can also influence sustainable practices on Earth. The need for efficient resource utilization in space provides a new perspective on waste, challenging us to reimagine it as a valuable resource rather than a byproduct to be discarded.

Genetically engineered crops, explored in Chapter 12, offer another cross-over potential. By creating crops designed to withstand harsh conditions, resist diseases, and provide enhanced nutritional value, we could address some of the challenges posed by climate change and growing global food demand.

Lastly, the psychological considerations of food in space mirror issues we see on Earth. The understanding we've gained about the importance of meal variety, cultural inclusivity, and the psychological comfort of food could influence the way we approach meal planning in settings such as schools, hospitals, and other institutions.

As we continue to reach for the stars, it's clear that the developments we make for life in space reverberate back to Earth. The research put into astro-food and space agriculture may one day become instrumental in addressing global challenges, making life more sustainable and perhaps even more flavorful here on our home planet. As we look to the future of cosmic cuisine, we can be assured that its impact will be felt as much on Earth as it is in space.

CHAPTER 18: KITCHEN OF THE COSMOS: WHAT A SPACE MEAL OF THE FUTURE MIGHT LOOK LIKE

As we have journeyed through the annals of space food, from the early tubes and freeze-dried packs of the Gemini and Apollo missions to the International Space Station's thermostabilized meals and attempts at space agriculture, one can't help but wonder: What might a space meal of the future look like? In this chapter, we delve into the potential developments and innovations that could shape the future of cosmic cuisine.

In envisioning the space meal of the future, we first consider the evolution of technology and its applications in food preparation. Already, we see the emergence of 3D food printing technologies, which could be tailored for use in space. Astronauts might one day input their food preferences into a system, and the 3D printer could then construct the meal from cartridges of food material, much like an inkjet printer but with edible 'inks.' This technology could offer a wide variety of foods prepared and customized to individual nutritional requirements and taste preferences.

A second innovation might come from cellular agriculture, where meat or other animal products are produced in-vitro without the need for traditional farming. With resources at a premium in space, cellular agriculture could provide a sustainable way to produce high-protein foods without the spatial and logistical challenges of raising livestock.

Looking further afield, as our ability to conduct space agriculture improves, meals might involve fresh ingredients grown right on spacecraft or extraterrestrial colonies. We've already seen the successful cultivation of lettuce and radishes in space; imagine preparing a meal with freshly harvested, space-grown vegetables.

It's not just the food itself that will evolve but also the way it's eaten. We are likely to see improvements in food packaging and eating utensils that make dining in microgravity more similar to the experience on Earth. Furthermore, as we consider long-duration space missions and the potential for multi-generational space travel, we must plan for dining areas that serve not just as places to consume food but also as social spaces, contributing to crew morale and mental health.

Of course, all these innovations must meet the central challenges of space food we've previously discussed: maintaining nutritional balance, long shelf-life, resistance to spoilage, and of course, palatability. The meal of the future will be more than just sustenance; it will be a feat of science and engineering, a morale booster, a taste of home, and perhaps even an interstellar culinary delight.

As we stand on the cusp of new space explorations – to Mars and beyond – the meal of the future remains to be fully defined. But one thing is for certain: cosmic cuisine will continue to evolve and surprise us, just as the infinite expanse of the universe does.

CHAPTER 19: DINING WITH THE STARS: ICONIC MEALS AND MEMORABLE SPACE FOOD MOMENTS

Space travel has gifted humanity with an array of iconic moments that we recall with awe, from the first moon landing to the breathtaking images of distant galaxies captured by the Hubble Space Telescope. Yet, some of the most memorable moments in space exploration are far more down-to-Earth, revolving around the act of eating. In this chapter, we will recount some of these iconic meals and memorable space food moments that have both delighted and grounded astronauts in the vast expanse of space.

Our journey starts with the earliest years of manned spaceflight, with John Glenn, the first American to orbit Earth, who famously dined on pureed beef and vegetables squeezed from an aluminum tube during his 1962 mission aboard Friendship 7. It was hardly gourmet, but it was the very first step in proving that humans could indeed eat and swallow in a microgravity environment.

Fast forward to 1972, during the Apollo 16 mission, when Charles

Duke and John Young sampled a variety of foods, including the much-debated 'cube meals,' which were bite-sized, freeze-dried meals vacuum-sealed in a special package. Upon landing on the moon, they became the first astronauts to eat on another celestial body.

Jumping to more recent times, the International Space Station (ISS) has hosted numerous memorable meal moments. From sharing a specially prepared canned roast quail during a joint Russian-American meal in 2001 to enjoying the first-ever 'space-grown' red romaine lettuce in 2015, the ISS has been the stage for many historic culinary firsts.

In 2018, Italian astronaut Paolo Nespoli missed his favorite food, pizza, so much that he mentioned it during a live broadcast. The crew was subsequently surprised by a specially prepared pizza kit delivered on a resupply mission, leading to the first-ever pizza party in space.

The tradition of celebrating Thanksgiving and Christmas with special meals continues on the ISS, reminding astronauts of their families and traditions back on Earth. These meals have included turkey, cranberry sauce, and even specially packaged eggnog.

Moreover, astronauts from various nations have brought pieces of their home cuisines to space. Japanese astronauts have enjoyed sushi, complete with wasabi, in microgravity, while Russian cosmonauts have dined on delicacies like tinned perch and borscht soup.

These iconic meals and memorable moments do more than just nourish the body; they serve as emotional anchors, providing comfort, sparking joy, and bridging cultural gaps in the unique environment of space. As we look to the future of space travel, it is clear that food will continue to play a pivotal role in our cosmic adventures, making space a little more like home.

CHAPTER 20: ADVANCED FOOD PRESERVATION TECHNIQUES FOR SPACE MISSIONS

The relentless pursuit of human space exploration has necessitated the evolution of various technologies, among which food preservation plays a pivotal role. Ensuring that astronauts are well-nourished during their missions, especially long-duration ones, is a challenge that extends beyond mere sustenance; it encompasses aspects of safety, psychology, and the complexity of life in microgravity.

Food Preservation: The Heart of Space Nutrition

In the realm of space travel, food preservation is not just about extending shelf life; it's about maintaining food safety, quality, and palatability in an environment where traditional methods of cooking and storing are infeasible. The unique challenges of space – such as limited storage, absence of refrigeration, and weight constraints – require innovative solutions.

High-Pressure Processing (HPP)

High-pressure processing, a method that utilizes extremely high pressure to destroy microorganisms in food, has emerged as a promising technology. HPP can effectively eliminate harmful bacteria while retaining the food's nutrients and taste, a crucial aspect for maintaining astronauts' health and morale. Unlike traditional thermal methods, HPP can process food at lower temperatures, which helps in preserving its sensory and nutritional quality.

Microwave-Assisted Thermal Sterilization (MATS)

Microwave-assisted thermal sterilization is another advanced technique gaining traction in space food preparation. MATS uses microwaves to rapidly heat packaged food, effectively destroying pathogens and extending shelf life. This method offers a significant advantage over conventional sterilization techniques, as it reduces the nutrient degradation typically associated with high-temperature processing.

Radiation Sterilization

Radiation sterilization, using gamma rays, electron beams, or X-rays, is a method that has been explored for space food preservation. It offers the advantage of penetrating packaging materials, ensuring sterility both inside and out. This method is particularly effective in inactivating microorganisms without the need for heat, thus preserving the food's texture and flavor.

Nutritional and Sensory Quality

Preservation methods must also consider the nutritional and sensory aspects of food. Astronauts require a diet rich in vitamins, minerals, and antioxidants, especially considering the increased radiation exposure and the unique stresses of space travel. Advanced preservation techniques aim to retain these essential nutrients, which might otherwise be lost through conventional processing methods.

The sensory quality of food – its taste, texture, and appearance – is equally important. Enjoyable food can have a significant positive impact on astronauts' psychological well-being. Techniques like HPP and MATS can maintain the original flavors and textures of food, making meals more appealing and palatable.

Packaging Innovations

Alongside preservation techniques, the packaging of space food plays a critical role. Advanced packaging materials are being developed to provide better protection against environmental factors such as moisture, oxygen, and cosmic radiation. These materials need to be lightweight yet robust, to withstand the rigors of space travel while ensuring the food's safety and quality.

Sustainability and Waste Management

Sustainability is another critical aspect. Given the limited resources in space, food preservation methods that utilize less energy and produce minimal waste are preferred. This not only conserves valuable resources but also aligns with the broader goals of sustainable space exploration.

The advancement of food preservation techniques for space missions is a multidimensional endeavor. It requires a meticulous balance between ensuring the safety and nutritional quality of food, maintaining its sensory attributes, and aligning with the sustainability objectives of space missions. As we venture further into space, the continuous evolution of these technologies will remain a cornerstone in the success of prolonged human presence beyond Earth.

CHAPTER 21: SPACE NUTRITION FOR CHILDREN AND ADOLESCENTS

The prospect of children and adolescents participating in space missions, whether for educational, research, or colonization purposes, raises critical considerations regarding their unique nutritional needs. These age groups are in their growth and development phase, which necessitates a tailored approach to their diet and nutrition, especially in the challenging environment of space.

Understanding the Unique Needs

Children and adolescents have different nutritional requirements from adults, primarily due to their growing bones, developing muscles, and rapidly changing endocrine systems. In the microgravity environment of space, these developmental processes could be impacted in unprecedented ways.

Growth and Development

The most significant difference in the nutritional needs of

younger astronauts compared to adults is their requirement for growth. Nutrients that support bone health, muscle growth, and overall physical development are crucial. This includes an increased need for proteins, calcium, vitamin D, and other minerals essential for bone health.

Metabolic Rates

Children and adolescents generally have higher metabolic rates than adults. This translates into higher caloric needs relative to their body size. In space, where physical activity might be reduced due to the microgravity environment, balancing these caloric needs with the risk of obesity or excessive weight gain becomes a challenge.

Cognitive Function and Development

Young brains are still developing and require a rich supply of nutrients to support cognitive functions. Omega-3 fatty acids, iron, zinc, and vitamins A, C, and D are critical for brain health. In the constrained environment of a spacecraft or space station, providing a diet rich in these nutrients is essential.

Challenges in Microgravity

The microgravity environment presents unique challenges to the human body, and these effects might be more pronounced in children and adolescents.

Bone Density and Muscle Mass

In microgravity, there is a known risk of decreased bone density and muscle mass due to the lack of gravitational force. For children and adolescents, whose bodies are in the crucial stages of bone and muscle development, this poses a significant risk. Ensuring an adequate intake of vitamin D and calcium becomes even more critical in space.

Fluid Distribution

In space, fluids tend to distribute more towards the upper body, which could impact various physiological processes. The dietary intake needs to be managed to ensure proper hydration while avoiding issues related to fluid imbalance.

Nutritional Strategies

Developing nutritional strategies for children and adolescents in space involves careful planning, considering the availability of food resources and the limitations of space travel.

Diverse and Nutrient-Dense Diet

The diet should be diverse and nutrient-dense, focusing on providing all the necessary vitamins and minerals for growth and development. Incorporating a variety of fruits, vegetables, whole grains, lean proteins, and dairy or dairy alternatives is key.

Addressing Palatability

Younger individuals might have different taste preferences compared to adults. Ensuring that the food is palatable and appealing is crucial to encourage adequate consumption and prevent nutritional deficiencies.

Supplements and Fortified Foods

Given the potential limitations in fresh food availability, supplements and fortified foods could play a significant role in meeting the nutritional needs of younger astronauts. These could include vitamin and mineral supplements, protein powders, and fortified snack bars.

Research and Future Directions

Ongoing research is essential to understand fully and address the unique nutritional needs of children and adolescents in space. This includes studying the effects of microgravity on their developing bodies and developing food systems that can sustain them on potential long-duration missions or space colonization endeavors.

As we advance towards the possibility of including younger populations in space missions, a comprehensive understanding and careful planning of their nutritional needs become paramount. This will ensure not only their physical health and well-being but also the success of future space missions involving these younger astronauts.

CHAPTER 22:
CULINARY TRAINING
FOR ASTRONAUTS

Embarking on a journey to space entails more than just scientific and technical training; it also includes mastering the art of cooking in a microgravity environment. Culinary training for astronauts is an essential aspect of space mission preparation, ensuring that they can effectively manage and prepare their meals while in orbit or on extraterrestrial surfaces.

The Importance of Culinary Skills in Space

Culinary training for astronauts goes beyond the basics of food preparation. In space, the act of cooking and eating takes on additional dimensions due to the unique environmental challenges.

Adapting to Microgravity

The absence of gravity significantly alters the cooking process. Liquids behave differently, and foods don't cook or boil in the same way as they do on Earth. Astronauts must learn techniques to handle food and liquids in a way that prevents them from floating away and potentially damaging equipment or contaminating the spacecraft.

Nutritional Balance

Astronauts need to understand the nutritional content of their meals. Given the constraints of space travel, including limited physical activity and the effects of microgravity on the body, maintaining a balanced diet is crucial for their health and well-being. Astronauts are trained in understanding the nutritional value of their food and how to combine different items to meet their dietary needs.

Psychological Significance

In the confined and isolated environment of space, mealtime serves as a crucial psychological anchor, providing comfort and a sense of normalcy. Culinary training includes preparing meals that are not only nutritious but also psychologically satisfying, taking into account personal preferences and cultural diversity.

Training Regimen

The culinary training regimen for astronauts involves several key components, tailored to the demands of space cuisine.

Basic Cooking Skills

Astronauts are trained in basic cooking skills, adapted for space conditions. This includes the use of specialized space kitchen equipment, such as rehydration stations and microwave ovens designed for microgravity.

Menu Planning

Training also involves planning menus that are nutritionally balanced, taking into consideration the duration of the mission and the storage life of different food items. Astronauts learn to select meals that provide the necessary calories, proteins, vitamins, and minerals.

Food Safety

Food safety is a critical aspect of the training. Astronauts learn about the risks of foodborne illnesses in space and how to handle and store food safely. They are trained in the sterilization processes and how to check for spoilage, a key aspect in an environment where traditional signs of food spoilage may not be as apparent.

Emergency Food Preparation

Astronauts are also prepared for emergency situations where regular food supplies might be compromised. They learn about using emergency rations and how to make the best use of available resources in case of supply shortages or equipment failures.

Future Directions

As space missions become longer and potentially involve deeper space exploration, the culinary training of astronauts will continue to evolve. The development of space agriculture and the potential for cooking with fresh produce grown in space habitats will add new dimensions to their training. Additionally, cultural and personal food preferences will play a larger role as the astronaut corps becomes more diverse.

Culinary training is a vital component of an astronaut's preparation for space missions. It equips them with the skills needed not only to nourish their bodies but also to maintain their morale and psychological health, which are just as critical for the success of long-duration space missions. As we continue to explore the cosmos, the art and science of cooking in space will evolve, reflecting the innovative spirit of human space exploration.

CHAPTER 23: ETHICAL CONSIDERATIONS IN SPACE AGRICULTURE

As humanity ventures further into space, agriculture in extraterrestrial environments becomes not only a scientific and technological challenge but also an area replete with ethical considerations. These considerations span a wide range of topics, from the sustainability of such endeavors to the broader implications for Earth and space environments.

Sustainability and Resource Use

One of the primary ethical concerns in space agriculture is sustainability. The notion of sustainability in space agriculture extends beyond the mere ability to grow food in space; it encompasses the efficient use of resources and minimal environmental impact. The use of microorganisms in life-support systems, as indicated by research, shows potential in enhancing the recycling of resources and loop-closure, thus promoting sustainability in space habitats. Additionally, this approach could have implications for Earth, particularly in harsh or remote environments, potentially improving food security and agricultural practices in these areas.

Genetic Modification and Biodiversity

The adaptation of plants for space environments often involves genetic modifications to enhance their resilience and nutrient use efficiency. For instance, genetic modifications have been proposed to enhance plant nutrient absorption and metabolism, optimizing resource efficiency crucial for space agriculture. While these modifications are promising for space agriculture, they raise ethical questions about biodiversity, genetic diversity, and potential long-term ecological impacts.

Equity and Access

The extension of agricultural practices to outer space also brings to light issues of equity and access. The history of agricultural technological innovation, starting from the green revolution, has often led to increased yields but also to ecological degradation and social inequalities. In space agriculture, similar concerns arise regarding who has access to these technologies and the benefits derived from them. There is a need to ensure that advancements in space agriculture do not exacerbate existing inequalities but rather contribute to equitable solutions both in space and on Earth.

Impact on Indigenous Communities and Traditional Practices

Expanding agricultural technologies to outer space should not overlook the importance of indigenous communities and traditional agricultural practices. It's crucial to consider how these new technologies might intersect with, and potentially impact, indigenous food sovereignty and traditional agricultural knowledge.

Ethical Framework for Space Exploration

Developing an ethical framework for space exploration, including agriculture, requires a multidisciplinary approach. It should integrate insights from science, technology, ethics, and social sciences to address the complex challenges and ensure responsible stewardship of space resources. The framework should consider the long-term implications of space agriculture on both extraterrestrial environments and Earth.

The ethical considerations in space agriculture are complex and multifaceted. They require careful deliberation and a holistic approach that takes into account sustainability, biodiversity, equity, and the impact on traditional practices. As we progress in our endeavors to grow food in space, it is imperative to develop responsible and ethical approaches that benefit not only space exploration but also contribute positively to challenges faced on Earth.

CHAPTER 24: THE FINAL FRONTIER: PREDICTIONS FOR THE FUTURE OF COSMIC CUISINE

As our journey through "Cosmic Cuisine" draws to a close, it's time to cast our gaze forward to the exciting and unknown landscape of the future. Armed with the insights gained in the preceding chapters, we're poised to explore the tantalizing possibilities that lie ahead for astronaut food and space agriculture.

The next generation of space food technology is likely to be profoundly influenced by advances in several interdisciplinary fields. From synthetic biology to nanotechnology and from materials science to artificial intelligence, the convergence of these technologies promises a future of cosmic cuisine that is more diverse, sustainable, and enjoyable.

Lab-grown meat and cellular agriculture, for example, could provide a viable solution to the challenge of producing animal proteins in space without the resource-intensive requirements of raising livestock. This could revolutionize the way astronauts receive necessary protein, making dishes featuring chicken, beef, or fish feasible without the logistical problems of storage and spoilage.

The field of 3D printing, already demonstrating its value in producing equipment on-demand aboard the ISS, might soon extend its reach into the kitchen of the cosmos. This technology could be used to print a wide range of foods with customized shapes, textures, and nutritional profiles. It's a technology that could transform a packet of nutrient-rich 'ink' into a delicious, visually appealing steak or strawberry at the touch of a button.

Hydroponic and aeroponic systems will likely become even more sophisticated, allowing a wider variety of crops to be grown. Coupled with advances in genetically engineered crops that can withstand the harsh conditions of space, we might see mini-farms on spacecraft or space stations that provide fresh, nutritious produce for the crew.

Nutritional science will continue to evolve, helping us understand how the human body's dietary needs may change in the unique environments of the moon, Mars, or deep space. This will help optimize astronaut diets for health, performance, and well-being, potentially even allowing for personalized nutrition plans based on an individual's genetics and gut microbiome.

Artificial intelligence and machine learning could be employed to manage these complex systems efficiently, from monitoring plant health and optimizing growth conditions to personalizing meals for each crew member based on their nutritional needs, personal preferences, and even their current mood.

As space travel opens up to more people through commercial

ventures, we can also expect an increased emphasis on the dining experience. Meals will not just be about sustenance and nutrition but also about enjoyment, comfort, and making the alien feel familiar. In that sense, the future of cosmic cuisine might be as much about psychology and culture as it is about biology and technology.

These are bold predictions, and the path forward won't be without its challenges. But, as we've seen throughout this book, humanity's ingenuity rises to meet the demands of exploration. In the cosmic kitchen, as in the wider universe, the only limit is our imagination. So, let us journey forth into the final frontier, armed with fork and knife, to boldly dine where no one has dined before.

APPENDIX A: GLOSSARY OF SPACE NUTRITION AND RELATED TERMS

1. **Microgravity**: A condition in space where the force of gravity is much weaker than on Earth, significantly affecting bodily functions and processes, including digestion and nutrient absorption.

2. **Hydroponics**: A method of growing plants in a water-based, nutrient-rich solution, without soil, often used in space agriculture due to the absence of gravity.

3. **Aeroponics**: A plant-cultivation technique where roots are suspended in the air and periodically misted with nutrients, suitable for space due to its efficient use of space and resources.

4. **Radiation Sterilization**: A food preservation method using ionizing radiation, essential in space to maintain food safety without traditional refrigeration methods.

5. **Bone Density Loss**: A significant health issue in space, due to the lack of gravitational force, necessitating a diet rich in calcium and vitamin D.

6. **Muscle Atrophy**: The reduction in muscle mass due to

the microgravity environment, requiring higher protein intake for astronauts.

7. **Closed-Loop Life Support System**: A system that recycles all waste products back into food, water, and oxygen; crucial for long-duration space missions.

8. **Bioregenerative System**: A system that integrates biological processes, like plant growth, into life support systems, for oxygen production and water purification.

9. **Nutrient Density**: The concentration of essential nutrients in food relative to its energy content, particularly important in space nutrition to minimize cargo weight and volume.

10. **Freeze-Drying**: A process to preserve food by freezing it and then reducing the surrounding pressure to allow the frozen water in the food to sublimate directly from the solid phase to the gas phase.

Understanding these terms is essential for grasping the complexities of maintaining astronaut health and well-being during space missions.

APPENDIX B: NUTRITIONAL REQUIREMENTS FOR DIFFERENT TYPES OF SPACE MISSIONS

The nutritional requirements for space missions vary depending on the mission type and duration, ranging from low-Earth orbit missions, like those to the International Space Station (ISS), to deep space missions, including potential trips to Mars.

Low-Earth Orbit Missions (e.g., ISS)

- **Safety and Stability**: The ISS food system is meticulously tested and processed on Earth to ensure safety. The food, including that grown aboard the spacecraft, is subject to rigorous microbial testing to minimize foodborne illness risks.

- **Variety and Enjoyment**: Maintaining the palatability of food is crucial. A variety of appetizing dishes are transported to the ISS to ensure astronauts enjoy their meals, which is vital for their health and well-being.

- **Nutritional Balance**: Essential nutrients are critical for the proper functioning of the body. The ISS food system is designed to provide a balanced diet to prevent nutritional deficiencies.

Mars and Deep Space Missions

- **Long-Term Stability**: For missions to Mars, where resupply is not possible, food systems must ensure stability for years. This requires advanced preservation techniques to maintain nutrition and quality over extended periods.
- **Self-Sufficiency**: The necessity to become more Earth-independent calls for an understanding of food production in space, not just transporting food from Earth.
- **Resource Minimization**: Limitations in resources such as water, power, and space mean that the food system must be efficient and minimize waste production.

General Criteria for Space Mission Food Systems

- **Food Safety**: Cleanliness and testing are paramount to reduce the risk of illness.
- **Nutritional Adequacy**: The food system must provide all essential nutrients in appropriate quantities to prevent health problems due to deficiencies.
- **Palatability**: Enjoyable food is crucial for ensuring adequate consumption, supporting astronaut health, and morale.

Future Directions

As space exploration progresses, the food systems for missions will need to evolve. This includes enhancing the quality of space food, developing more sustainable and efficient production and recycling processes, and ensuring the food meets the complex nutritional needs of astronauts in varying space environments. Continuous research and development are essential for these advancements.

Note: This summary is derived from a comprehensive review of existing knowledge and findings in the field of space nutrition, with inputs from intramural and extramural experts. As knowledge in this area expands and evolves, so too will the approaches to nutrition in space missions.

APPENDIX C: OVERVIEW OF SPACE NUTRITION RESEARCH INSTITUTIONS AND PROGRAMS

Space nutrition research is a multidisciplinary field involving several leading institutions and programs. Key organizations in this domain include:

1. **NASA's Space Food Systems Laboratory (SFSL)**: Located at the Johnson Space Center in Houston, Texas, the SFSL is central to the research and development of nutritious and high-quality meals for space missions. The laboratory is responsible for the production, development, and packaging of flight food for NASA programs, including the International Space Station (ISS), Orion Multi-Purpose Crew Vehicle, and Commercial Crew Program. It also houses the Advanced Food Technology research team, focusing on future missions beyond low-Earth orbit.

2. **Space Food Research Facility (SFRF)**: Based in College

Station, Texas, the SFRF supports the development of flight food and menus, packaging, and food-related hardware. It produces heat-stabilized foods in pouches and develops innovative food processing techniques.

3. **NASA's Advanced Food Technology (AFT) Project**: This project defines food systems for future missions, emphasizing long-duration exploration missions. The AFT project addresses the challenges of providing safe, nutritious, and palatable food for missions lasting up to five years.

These institutions and programs are at the forefront of space nutrition research, addressing the unique challenges of providing safe, nutritious, and enjoyable food for astronauts in space. Their work not only advances human space exploration but also contributes to food technology and nutrition science on Earth.

THE END

Printed in Great Britain
by Amazon

37172257R00056